WITHDRAWN

· AUTUMN WILLOWS

AUTUMN WILLOWS

Poetry by Women
of China's Golden Age

Translated from the original Chinese
by
Bannie Chow, M.A.

Thomas Cleary, Ph.D.

Story Line Press
2003

Published by Story Line Press, Three Oaks Farm, PO Box 1240, Ashland, OR 97520-0055
www.storylinepress.com.

This publication was made possible thanks in part
to the generous support of the Nicholas Roerich Museum,
the Louis Dreyfus Holding Company Inc. and our individual contributors.

Cover design by Sharon McCann
Book design by Lysa McDowell
Cover art: "Autumn," Asian Art Museum of San Francisco, Collection
of Master Chao Shao-an, 1992.269. Reproduced by permission.

ISBN 1-58654-025-4
Library of Congress Cataloging-in-Publication Data
Autumn willows : poetry by women of China's golden age / Translated from
the original Chinese by Bannie Chow and Thomas Cleary.
p. cm.
ISBN 1-58654-025-4
1. Chinese poetry--Women authors--Translations into English. 2.
Chinese poetry--Tang dynasty, 618-907--Translations into English. I.
Title: Poetry by women of China's golden age. II. Chow, Bannie, 1948-
III. Cleary, Thomas. IV. Li, Ye, 8th cent. Poems. English. V. Xue, Tao,
768-831. Poems. English. VI. Yu, Xuanji, 842-872. Poems. English.
PL2658.E3 A87 2003
895.1'130809287--dc21
2003011249

To the memory of the poetesses
of all times and places

CONTENTS

Poems by Xue Tao

Poems by Yu Xuanji

Foreword

Poetry and song, loved by all peoples, are among the most basic timbers of human civilization, found everywhere and raised to high degrees of refinement in the great cultures of ancient Africa, India and Asia. The heart and mind of China, the oldest living civilization in the world, have been nurtured for millennia by feelings and ideas captured in the gossamer nets of poetry and song.

Ancient Chinese sages taught poetry and song for the cultivation and refinement of emotions, but word-music also came to conceal many other treasures as well, treasures of knowledge, of wisdom and of spirituality.

The long, convoluted history of China is marked by a succession of imperial dynasties, each with its own political and cultural identity. The apogee of Chinese civilization, the golden age of China's culture, was reached in the glorious Tang dynasty (618–905 C.E.). Steeped in the brilliant literary and spiritual milieu of the era, Tang dynasty poetry stands out as an advanced art, highly refined yet still youthful and robust even as it reached a distinguished maturity.

Among the greatest poets of the Tang were a number of women whose work gained highest acclaim even in the lofty atmosphere of the magnificent cosmopolitan Tang culture.

Although it was a patriarchal society, in Tang China women were considerably freer than in later times. Women could divorce on their own initiative, divorcées and widows could freely remarry, and married women might have paramours. Although excluded from the civil service system, many women were educated and literate. The barbaric custom of foot-binding, for a thousand years the arch symbol of suppression of women, had not yet been invented in the Tang dynasty.

It was in this setting that three of the greatest poetesses of China, perhaps of the world, lived and worked. The sheer beauty of their poetry bespeaks the richness of their inner and outer world, yet the poignant tragedy of their lives also tells of the shadows that were to destroy the Tang civilization and enshroud China in centuries of ever-growing militarism and repression.

Li Ye, Xue Tao, and Yu Xuanji all lived in the mid Tang dynasty. Li Ye was a Taoist priestess, said to have been comely, calm, artistic, and musical. Li Ye was also forthright and fearlessly critical of the powers that be; as a result, very few of her poems have been preserved. According to one of the typically sparing accounts of her life, Li Ye was ultimately murdered at the order of the emperor.

Xue Tao was sold into slavery as an entertainer in government service. Originally from a free family of the capital city, the exceptionally talented Xue Tao was taken into slavery as a girl when her father fell on hard times. Sent to various places to entertain military leaders, Xue Tao is said to have served in no less than eleven satrapies and matched verses with many of the greatest poets of the time. In spite of the many hardships she endured, Xue Tao lived to the age of seventy-five.

Yu Xuanji, also a Taoist priestess, is perhaps the most famous and most tragic of the famous poetesses. Ravishingly beautiful and exquisitely sensitive, she entered Taoist orders at the age of sixteen. Her remarkable poetry attracted the attention of the literati, and she had a number of lovers from among the intelligentsia.

Pursued by countless other suitors, however, including many unworthy individuals, she eventually despaired and turned, it is said, to Sapphic love. In a story that, like much of official Chinese history, is biased and improbable in the detail and manner of its telling, the priestess was ultimately accused and convicted of beating her maid and alleged lover to death in a fit of rage, and was herself summarily executed while still a young woman.

Because the massive oppression of women in China snowballed after the fall of the Tang dynasty and the rise of military hegemons, the lurid tale of Yu's death is remembered even when her exquisite poetry is forgotten, compounding the tragedy of her judicial murder for many generations to come. Later Chinese scholars and Confucian historians, serving the interests of the ruling elites, obviously could not cope with the images of free women like these Taoist priestesses. The songs of parting and longing that mark the works of these great poetesses of Tang are therefore not simply mirrors of personal feeling; poignant, artful, and yet austere, filled with hidden insights, they are like autumn willows, farewells to an era of innocent joy.

Poems by Li Ye

Springtime Bedroom Lament

The fruits are red already
on the peach trees over the rail,
the peach trees there surrounding
the hundred fathom well.
I think of you up north,
sent off to the war,
leaving me behind
perhaps forever more.

From a Sickbed,
Rejoicing in a Friend's Arrival

Many were frosty moons in the past;
now I suffer in fog and mist.
Although I get to meet you
I'm still sick abed;
even as I try to greet you
tears fall first instead.
Urged to drink the wine of Tao,
I respond with a verse you may know.
By accident we're tipsy now;
where else is there to go?

Parting on a Moonlit Night

Silent shines the moon on lovers
speechless as they part;
light is in the lunar orb,
feelings are in the heart.
The longing of lovers separated
is like the light of the moon;
it pierces the clouds
and rides the waters
to the beloved's room.

Sending off a Friend

Whenever my gaze falls on the willows,
the sorrow of parting will always be there.
Endless, the waters of West River;
how will your lone boat fare?
Even the tide only reaches so far;
after a point, news must be rare.
Messenger birds will nonetheless fly;
year after year, again they will try.

Willows

I love most the slender willows
along the winding stream;
the evening sun shifts their shadows
over the aquamarine.
The eastern breeze colors the world
again with its yearly green;
a traveler abroad is saddened more
by the distance from home this spring.
Low hanging leaves already hide
oars plied along the shore;
the upper branches are shutting in
the people on upper floors.
Their graceful trunks tapering,
they make a beautiful scene,
scattering blossoms like cotton
on a bed of emerald green.

A Taoist Message to an Official

Don't get attached
to fame that won't last;
better to trim
bureaucrat's whims.
A century's like a day and a night;
things of the past are now gone from sight.
Worry streaks the hair with grey,
yet a youthful face is not all the way;
nowhere's better than India
where you can resort to old Buddha.

To a Friend in the Secretariat

In this peaceful province
the year is coming to an end;
I wonder how your offices are
when they are empty then.
The distant waters buoy
the rafts of the immortals;
cold stars accompany
the chariots of officials.
When you pass by
the Cliff of Giant Thunder
don't forget these few lines
I've written in my letter.

On Receiving a Letter

Into my looking glass
I moodily gaze,
lazily combing my hair;
in the evening rain
and whistling wind
my garden trees grow bare.
It's no wonder I weep on seeing
your fine calligraphy;
it's only because I'm sad to be reading
a letter from you to me.

Rose Blossoms

Green stems merging
with crimson blossoms
have no strength to stand;
leaning over the balustrade,
they seem to show their pride.
Deepest folds the finest,
their scent lures butterflies;
picking them, beware the flames
of their springtime fire.
Skillfully weaving a delicate veil
in the open air,
on the ground they spread a quilt
like brocade lying there.
They're best viewed
at early dawn,
covered with the dew;
out my window, emerald draped,
another blooms anew!

To a Friend

Gazing over the waters,
I try to climb the peaks;
lofty are mountains,
and broad indeed the lakes.
In our thoughts of longing
there's no day or night;
months and years have passed
as we wish and wait.
Densely green, the mountain wood
flourishes in splendor;
soft as cotton, the wildflowers
blossom in the fields.
My feelings are boundless
since we've been apart;
when we get to meet,
I'll tell you my heart.

Saying Goodbye

Formally bidding farewell,
meeting each other to part,
the sadness of separation
tugs ever more at the heart.
The river runs three thousand miles;
where will your lonesome boat moor?
Where the tide doesn't reach,
news will be scarce
from a far, far distant shore.
Only the wild geese will return,
migrating year after year.

Making Paper Fish for a Friend

Letters like leftover snow
folded and knotted and lo!
—a pair of paper carp!
So if you want to know
what's inside my heart,
look at the letters below
the undersides of the carp.

While Living Alone

Off in the floating clouds,
my heart is far away,
how do I know you might
never come back some day?
The clouds of my heart
have gathered between
being and nothingness;
why in the world does the crazy wind
kick up such a fuss,
raging at the mountains south
and the mountains north?

To a Friend

Gazing over the waters,
I tried ascending the mountain;
the mountain was high
and the lake was wide.
I think of you
day and night;
I've looked to you
year after year.
The mountain woods
are thick and dense,
meadow flowers bloom
in a boundless expanse.
After parting,
there's endless emotion,
when we meet,
a moment of joy.

A Temporary Farewell

A flowing stream
outside the city gates,
a lone boat
in the setting sun.
Emotions of parting
pervade the fragrant grasses
growing thickly all around.
While my dreams are roaming
a special garden,
you are gone
to a distant valley.
When you come back,
let's meet again;
don't wander off
with a young siren.

The Bitterness of Longing

Deep is the ocean of human life,
but the ocean has a shore;
twice as deep is my longing for you,
and longing is ever more.
Lute in hand, I go upstairs,
but there is no one here;
moonlight fills the empty room,
shining from way out there.
Plucking my lute, I play a tune,
Song of Pining for You;
a string snaps as it rends my heart,
breaking it in two.

Eight Superlatives

Furthest and nearest are east and west;
deepest and most shallow
are pure clear valley streams.
Highest and brightest are the sun and moon;
closest and most distant are husband and wife.

Feeling Excitement

Morning clouds and evening rain
follow one another again;
people come by, geese fly away,
each to return some day.
The jade pillow only knows
an endless stream of tears that flows;
useless is the silver lamp's shine
through these sleepless nights of mine.
Gazing up at the bright moonlight
I'm filled with thoughts tonight;
looking down to view the river,
I have a message to deliver.
I remember when I first heard
the Phoenix Pavilion Song;
it made me feel so peaceful then,
and yet it made me long.

Poems by Xue Tao

Wind

The breeze upon the fragrant grass
has now passed far away,
the harpstrings of a whirlwind
raise a plaintive cry.
The rustle of the falling leaves
can be heard in the forest, near;
along the pine-lined pathway,
the night is chillingly clear.

Cicadas

The clear, pure sounds of dripping dew
carry far away;
withered leaves blown by the wind
pile up day by day.
The chirping of each insect
seems to join with the rest,
even if every one of them
has a separate nest.

Spring Views

I

When the flowers blossom,
not all enjoy them alike;
and when the blossoms drop,
not all lament them alike.
If you wonder
who is longing for whom,
you see when the flowers drop
and see when they bloom.

2

I gather sweet grasses to tie
the bond of our hearts' communion,
using this as a gift
to give to an intimate friend.
Just as springtime sorrow
seemed about to depart,
the birds of spring call sadly again,
tearing at my heart.

3
Days of zephyrs and blossoms
are coming to an end;
and still my wedding day would seem
indefinitely postponed.
Yet to meet a man
with whom I have one heart,
in vain I bind the tie
that shows we'd never part.

4
Though the flowers may be
blooming everywhere,
that just makes
the both of us long;
in the morning mirror I face,
streams of jade tears
trickle down.
O zephyr of spring,
do you know,
or is my sorrow unknown?

A Pair of Birds on a Lake

A pair of birds come to rest
on a pond of aquamarine;
in the mornings they fly away,
and in the evenings return.
Reminiscent of when the hen
had fledglings in her care,
their hearts join in communion
in their lotus leaf lair.

Parting

When the flowers fall
from the parasol trees,
the phoenix parts
from its mate and leaves.
Whenever I think of you
crossing the great northern ridges,
here in my heart I feel
colder, more frigid.
A beauty may present a poem
as a farewell gift,
but in fully half of the lyrics
mourning and loss are mixed.

A Message

The mansions of the wizards
are shrouded in the fog;
when the mists open, you see into
the palace of the gods.
The spirit immortals from heaven above
praise remaining on earth below
working for the world.

Mountain Dawn:
To a Friend

The first turn of the sunlight orb
illumines immortals' doors;
then whirls on through the misty wind
into the darkness above.
Though I cannot get to share
this morning view with you,
the azure on the horizon expands,
spreading blue upon blue.

Ode to Riverside Willows

Emerald green extends along
the desolate river shore;
misty figures hazily drift
into a building afar.
Shadows spread over the face
of the autumn water;
there where the fisherman stands,
falling flowers scatter.
The ancient roots of the willows
make lairs where fishes hide;
the branches hang down low enough
for travelers' boats to be tied.
It's a stormy night,
with gusting wind and rain;
a frightful dream awakens me
and makes me sad again.

To Ministry President Liu

When you stopped a stalwart army,
songs of triumph filled the streets;
with March rain falling on the river,
hundreds of blossoms herald the spring.
The prisons have long been empty,
the weaponry's covered with dust:
Confucian scholars and Buddhist monks
watch performers singing;
travelers stopping lie at ease
on scarlet bolsters drinking.
Brush and inkstone ready at hand,
poetry books surround my chair;
you have been so attentive to me,
I could be your protegée.

Sending off a Friend (1)

Here's an early autumn branch
from the countless river willows;
the wind has changed on the delicate earth,
but the colors haven't yet faded.
I'm going to break this willow branch
as a gift to you on parting,
please don't let the misty moonlight
cause us both to sorrow.

Mandarin Duck Flowers

Their verdant splendor fills
the scented stairs of stone;
like little mandarin ducks, in pairs
the inner petals have grown.
Let us just enjoy how long
the pleasant spring days last;
never mind the autumn wind,
though it comes on fast.

Sending off a Friend (2)

New reeds grow in the wetlands,
nightfall brings the frost;
the moonlight cold
and the mountain colors
join in the deepest green.
Who says that your journey
must begin tonight?
Lonely dreams are far away
as the long road to the border.

To Prime Minister Gao,
After Pacification of a Rebellion

Startled to see the land
so desolate and poor,
I glimpse the verdant hills to see
the setting sun of yore;
now I trust your majesty
to bring light as before;
even sun and moon above
take radiance from yours.

Thoughts of Home

Below the sacred Mount Omei
the river's quiet flow
takes pity on my heart, so like
an untied boat, unmoored.
When did the lonely sail
depart the brocade ford?
From midstream, in unison,
drifts the sound of oars.

Reply to a Verse
Received in Person from a Statesman

You handled the problems masterfully
in your test on strategic arts;
will we ever meet again
and open up our hearts?
I beg to ask, for whom
is the scenery so fine:
Deep in the misty haze, wispy willows
trail streamers of emerald green.

Plum Blossoms

The master painter's orchard scene
moves into the blossoming trees,
just at the time when spring rains
come back to the valley's east.
It's late in the day, the oriole cries,
but what can be done about these?
Crimson makeup, thick and thin,
lies heavy on the trees.

Atop a Mountain

Even in a master painting
the sense of a mountain's grandeur
is after all nothing more
than ink set down on paper;
now that I'm actually here on high,
gazing abroad from up in the sky,
my headdress, with its trailing pearls
crowns a thousand peaks.

Chrysanthemum Festival Rain

I

A startling wind is storming
as far as the eye can see,
a gale profoundly steeped
in northerly energy.
The river city is desolate,
dark and gloomy by day;
who cares if we cannot go
climbing the mountain this way?
Still the chrysanthemums, though,
are fragrant in the cold;
too bad we cannot view them,
colorful as gold!

2

It's the autumn dogwood festival,
but the holiday's dispirited.
Chrysanthemums of gold,
flowering in the cold,
are giving off a scent

that permeates the hall.
I realize now the goddess
intends to come around;
she's first made the clouds and rain
darken the banks of the pond.

By the River

All of a sudden the west wind declares
geese on the wing, flying in pairs,
while in the human world down here,
from nowhere mind and body appear.
If not for the thought of a letter
carried by a fish,
who could stand by the river
every night with a wish?

To Inspector Zheng

Rain darkens Eyebrow Mountain,
the river water flows;
in a high tower, wrapped in long sleeves
someone stands apart.
A pair of banners, a thousand horsemen
clog the eastern streets;
there is just one lady alone
who looks beyond it all.

Myriad Mile Bridge,
Reply to a Friend in Government

At Myriad Mile Bridge alone
I sing a song of long lost home;
who knows if words can ever express
the sadness I feel inside my chest.
The grace of a good government
is a match for that of yore;
not only can it be like a ship,
but also like rain,
a refreshing downpour.

Aronia valley

Springtime makes the scenery
retain a mystical fog;
the fishes on the water's face
are all in flowery garb.
The human world doesn't think
of difference in spiritual plants;
everyone uses crimson dye
to stain their silken floss.

Lotus-Picking Boats

Like leaves before the wind
they press through lily and lotus,
both finding some fish and sending
another new autumn's notice.
Time goes by, the people talk,
conversing in soft tones;
the valley river fills with red sleeves
as the rowing song begins.

Water Chestnuts and Floating Hearts

The water vegetable floating hearts
is dragging at an angle,
greenery floating up buoyant;
the willow threads
along with their leaves
lie down in the clear pure current.
When will I ever get to behold
the valley river source?
Picking the water chestnut blossoms,
I sail my boat on its course.

Gold Lantern Flowers

By the rails I cannot see
all that many leaves;
over the steps there tumble
gorgeous flowers in sheaves.
Looking closely, what can compare
to this scenery, so pretty?
Morning mist massing anew
'round the shrine over Crimson City.

Countryside Views in Springtime,
To a Friend

1
Lowered head, a long, long time
I stand before the rose;
I love it like the orchids
whose scent gets in your clothes.
Why is it that we're apart,
like birds gone from the nest,
separated, flown away,
one gone east, one west?

2
This morning I let my eyes
play on the wildflowers;
I stick them in my topknot,
hide them in my apron,
strew them on my carpet.
Head full, sleeves full,
and with a bunch in my hand,
I let people know I'm back
from viewing flowers again.

Sent Far Away

1

The cotton-rose first drops its petals;
it's autumn in the mountains west.
My letters to you, open or sealed,
bespeak my heart's distress.
In my chamber, I know naught
of the matters of war;
the moon now high, I go upstairs
to watch for my man afar.

2

Growing at an even pace,
the supple sweet-flag's green;
it's late in spring, flowers fall
jamming the valley stream.
Thinking of you at the Pass of Chin,
I wonder if you've ridden by;
moonlight on a thousand doors,
I cover my face and cry.

A Spring in Autumn

Its cool color clears first;
the area's shrouded in mist.
A haunting tune drifts afar,
the sound of a ten-string harp.
Lying abed a long, long time,
I'm drawn by emotional thoughts
keeping one who's sorrowing
from sleeping half the night.

Ten Verses on Separation

I
A Dog Taken Away from its Master

Four or five years, it's used to cavorting
by the gates of scarlet lacquer,
fur perfumed, feet washed clean,
cared for by its master.
But then it happened to bite
a guest of the house, well-liked;
so now there's no more bed
on a carpet of red.

2
A Writing Brush out of the Hand

Only the finest stem
and the best of hair
together make a brush
that will suit one fair:
on paper graced with crimson lines

it scatters pearls
like flowers fine.
Just because of long time use
the point is worn, exhausted;
no longer is it taken up
by a writing master.

3
A Horse Taken from its Stable

Snowy ears, a ruddy coat,
hooves of light aquamarine—
daily east and west it would run,
fleet as one chasing the wind.
Startled, it bolted,
making the master fall;
and now its neigh's no longer heard
in its glamorous stall.

4
A Parrot Taken out of its Cage

Out northwest, isolated,
a solitary, alone,
flying here and there would light
atop a brocade cushion.
All because it spoke aloud
words devoid of tact,
never again from its cage
will it call anyone back.

5
A Sparrow Separated from its Nest

It frequented the scarlet gates,
never to be abandoned;
the master always liked its voice,
the way it used to chatter.
Carrying mud to build a nest,
it soiled a coral headrest;
no more will it make its house
up there in the rafters.

6

A Pearl Taken from the Palm

Inside and outside clear,
immaculate, round and bright,
like a shining crystal palace
it's radiant with light.
All on account of a single flaw,
perfection incomplete,
though once in the palm of the hand
it could not spend the night.

7

A Fish Taken out of a Pond

Four or five autumns it frolicked
in the lotus pond,
always shaking its scarlet tail
making sport of hook and line.
It happened to break a flower off,
now it can swim no more
in the pond of lotuses,
among the clear waves, pure.

8

A Falcon off the Wrist

Its talons sharp as sword points,
its eyes are just like bells;
catching rabbits on the plains
suits high spirits well.
For no reason it darted away
beyond the cloudy sky,
unable to alight again
on the wrist of royalty.

9

Bamboo Removed from an Inn

Newly planted in rows, four or five,
there was luxuriant growth;
always strong, it was able to bear
even the autumn frost.
Because the springtime shoots
pierced right through the wall,
no longer can its shadow
cover the jadelike hall.

10

A Mirror Taken from its Stand

Once out of the mold,
yellow gold
finally became a mirror;
first made, it was like
the full, round moon
coursing through the air.
Because it has been dirtied
and dust has covered it all,
it can't be mounted on a jade stand
in a luxurious hall.

On the Way Into Exile,
To Commander Wu

1

The firefly's in the wilds,
the moon is in the sky;
how can the firefly reach the moon,
how could it fly so high?
The sun and moon must shine on us both
though thousands of miles away;
I tear my gaze from the clouds above—
no message comes my way.

2

I draw the reins atop the ridge,
cold and getting colder;
a light wind and fine rain
pierce my heart and liver.
If only I could be allowed
to go back to my home,
I'd never look at a landscape screen
ever, ever again!

Poems by Yu Xuanji

Bedroom Lament

Fragrant grass fills her hands
as she weeps in the setting sun;
she heard that the neighbor's man
has just come back from the front.
Swans of the south
had only gone north
just the other day;
now northern geese
are flying south
on this morning, today.
Though spring comes
and autumn goes,
her feelings for him remain;
as autumn goes
and spring comes,
news from him is scarce.
The doors are closed
at this noble house;
no one ever comes:
What has made desolation
pierce the silken drapes?

Hearing a Friend Has Returned from a Fishing Trip

An endless stretch of lotuses—
their scent perfumes
my summer dress;
where have you been, my friend,
where have you sailed your boat?
I only regret I cannot be
one of the Mandarin ducks;
at least I'd be able to sit with you
by the shore where you cast your line.

A Conscientious Objector
Builds the Temple of Prosperity

A recluse creates a realm apart,
where travelers stop on their way;
anonymous writings are left on the walls,
the shrine has not yet been named.
He dug a pond, and a spring emerged;
he cleared the path, but the grass has regrown.
The lofty golden temple opens eyes wide,
bright and clear at the river's edge.

A Mist Enshrouded Inn

The spring flowers and autumn moon
make their way into poetry;
the bright days and clear nights
are themselves free immortals.
No need to roll up the beaded blind,
for it has never been lowered,
a single cot's been moved for good
to sleep in view of the mountains.

Early Autumn

Tender young chrysanthemums
are freshly tinged with color;
distant mountains, far away,
lock in the evening haze.
A cool breeze startles verdant trees,
pure melody's found in a crimson lute.
The lot of the longing wives
is the brocade in their looms;
the lot of the men at war
is the cold of foreign skies.
Though they try to correspond,
how will their letters arrive?

To an Awaited Friend
Held up by the Rains

How sad we have no chance to meet
although we've been in touch.
As I close the door,
it's bathed in the light of the moon;
when I raise the blind,
a drizzle's already begun.
The murmuring of a nearby spring
is heard by the staircase of stone;
while distant waves are swelling
down by the river's shore.
Thoughts of home bring sadness
to the traveler in autumn,
reciting lines of poetry
in a melancholy way.

Seeing the New Listing
of Successful Degree Candidates

Cloudy peaks fill the eyes,
far from the lightness of spring;
silver spools of calligraphy
take shape beneath my hand.
Too bad my silken woman's dress
obscures my poetry;
looking up, I uselessly
envy the names on the list I see.

Reply to a Friend

Though we live on the same street,
you haven't passed by all year.
Fine poetry pleased your former lady,
distinguished laurels, your new degree.
A Taoist nature cares not at all
for the cold of ice and snow,
a Buddhist heart laughs aloud
at ostentatious silk;
since you rose to rank at court,
we have no chance to meet—
having climbed to the lofty sky,
no more is there a way to receive
the misty waves below.

Summer Days in the Mountains

Ever since I moved here
to live the way immortals do,
clusters of flowers abound all around,
so planting is something I've never done.
The bushes in the yard
make hangers for my clothes;
the fresh spring by my sitting place
is a flowing cup of wine.
The balustrade fades into a path
through the deep bamboo;
my silken dress is surrounded
by books in disarray.
Leisurely boarding a pleasure boat,
I sing poems to the moon,
trusting in the gentle breeze
to blow me back to home.

Two Verses on Parting

1

These nights in our chamber of
love fulfilled your expectations;
hardly did I count
on you, my lover, parting.
Dozing off, I cannot tell
where the clouds have gone;
the moths of the wilds are flitting
'round the guttering lamp.

2

Water adapts unresisting
to the shape of the vessel it's in;
obviously a definite form
cannot be fixed for good.
Once the clouds have gone,
they have no mind to return.
Wistful in the springtime breeze
over the river of an eve,
a mandarin duck without its flock
flies away alone.

Visiting a Master Alchemist, Not Finding Him at Home

Where shall I look
for my spiritual friend?
An acolyte's at home alone—
the stove is warm,
the herbs still cooking;
a neighbor prepares
some boiled tea.
Dimly lamplight flickers
on the murals of the walls;
from the banner pole
in the setting sun
a shadow leaning falls.
Over and over I look around;
flowers beyond the walls!

To a Friend

Crickets are chirping
by the stepping stones;
mist and dew are clearing
in the garden boughs.
Music in the moonlight
makes a nearby echo;
seen from the upper chamber,
the distant hills are aglow.
A cold wind clings
to my bamboo mat,
the sorrow of my life
comes through my lute.
You're so late, my friend,
in writing;
what can soothe
this autumn longing?

To a New Neighbor,
Answering a Verse and Asking for Wine

Your poem's been delivered,
and recited a hundred times;
there's freshness in each letter,
as well as an elegant rhyme.
Since my neighbor wishes
to come and visit me,
can I remain remote, aloof
without a heart of stone?
Hopes of lovers meeting remote,
empty skies fill the eyes;
dreams of togetherness broken,
my lute's gone out of tune.
All the more in this wintry cold
I feel nostalgia for home;
if you've got wine like the sages of old,
please don't drink it alone.

Late Spring Impromptu

Living on a side street
in a house of poverty,
few are my companions
in this hidden alleyway;
only in the heart of dreams
is my beloved there.
Incense wafts into my silken dress,
where are they having a party?
The breeze carries with it the voice of song;
where is the pleasure pavilion?
The street is so near, I'm wakened at dawn
by the sound of noisy drumming,
my courtyard's so peaceful,
the magpies' chatter
scatters my springtime sorrows.
How can I pursue the affairs
that belong to the human world?
Remaining the same for ten thousand miles,
I never tie down my boat.

To a Neighbor Girl

The shyness of the daytime's covered
by a silken sleeve;
the melancholy of springtime makes it
hard to rise and dress.
A priceless gem's more easily found
than a man who has a heart.
Hidden tears on the pillow,
secret sorrows among the flowers;
if one could glimpse a righteous man,
why lament a mere playboy?

To an Intimate

No wine can wash away
the sorrow of separating;
nothing can unloose the knot
tied in my heart by parting.
The fragrant orchids, though faded away,
will return in the gardens of spring;
the willows to the east and west
furnish many a leisure-boat mooring.
Gathering only to disband is sad in itself already,
for clouds can never stay;
feelings should learn fluidity
a flowing river's way.
In the season of blossoming flowers,
we cannot meet, can we?
So I won't go on drinking languidly
in a land of fantasy.

To Master Scholar Li,
In Thanks for a Summer Mat

Your valued bamboo summer mat
newly graces my emerald tower,
cool as the deepest limpid pool
of the purest jadelike water,
but the feeling's like a beautiful fan,
lamenting too an early fall,
left on a silver bed.

To a Lover, Spring Feelings

The mountain trails are steep,
their rocky steps so dangerous,
and yet the pain of travel
is not the heart of my sorrow;
the pain is my longing for you.
Ice in distant valleys melting
moves me like your clear, crisp voice;
snow afar on the frigid peaks
reminds me of your handsome form.
Please don't listen to vulgar songs
and drink too much in spring;
avoid the company of idlers
who like to play chess all night.
Constant as pine,
not hard like a stone,
I pledge to be always here;
as birds of a feather
whose hearts are conjoined,
can our union be far?

Though I dislike traveling alone
all the winter day,
I know I can count on meeting you
when the moon is full.
And when I leave,
what can I give
for a suitable farewell?
Falling tears in the clear daylight—
a poem from me to you.

Melancholy Thoughts

I

Falling leaves scatter,
along with the evening rain;
sitting alone, I play the lute,
singing aloud to myself.
Letting go of emotions,
I no more resent
a lack of intimate friends;
nurturing nature,
I freely give up
the waves of the ocean of pain.
The carriages of rich men
clatter outside the door,
by my pillow, in contrast,
are many books on the Tao.
A commoner may at last
reach a high estate,
but time in the verdant mountains and rivers
only passes once.

2

Lamenting my sentimentality
is sad enough for me;
how much more
in windswept moonlight
filling my garden with fall!
My inner chamber is near enough
to hear the watchman's call;
night after night,
by the pale lamplight
I'm quietly going grey.

Rainbound in Autumn

Yellow chrysanthemums filling the yard
bloom beside the hedges;
ruddy cheeks in the looking glass
blush like scarlet blossoms.
Kept in by the wind and rain
on this autumn day,
I'd drink my fill of the golden cup
but know not where I may.

Mourning for Another

Fresh peaches I have seen
remind me of her delicate form;
in windswept willows I recognize
her feathery, moth-like brows.
The pearl has returned
to the dragon cave;
who will see her now?
The mirror's still here,
but the phoenix is gone;
how can they converse?
On misty rainy nights from now,
dreams will be of sorrow;
none can bear the silent pain
when desolate, alone.
The sun has set and disappeared
beyond the western slopes;
and now the moon has risen
over the eastern hills:
how bitter it is to think of how
the end can come without cause.

An Allegory

Rosy peaches everywhere
presenting the colors of spring,
on emerald willows at every house
the moonlight glow is agleam.
Freshly groomed, she awaits upstairs
the coming of the night;
in the bedroom, sitting alone,
she keeps her feelings inside.
Fishes frolic under the leaves
of the lotus flowers;
the twittering of sparrows calls
on the rainbow'd horizon.
Human life is but a dream,
a dream of joy and sorrow;
how can one be able to join
the company of immortals?

To Scholar Li,
A Melancholy View of the Yangtse River

A thousand limbs of maple leaves
and myriad branches more;
in the shadows of the bridges
evening sailboats linger.
Thinking of you, my heart
is like the torrent of the river,
flowing eastward day and night
never to rest in slumber.

Greeting Li Jinren

This day is one of happiness,
foretold by news of joy;
last night I read the tidings
under the lamplight's glow.
Perfuming the air with incense,
I step outside to greet you,
no envy for the lovers of old
at their rendezvous.

Clearing My Mind

At leisure, free, no duty mine,
I roam the landscape alone:
cutting through the clouds, there shines,
over the river, the moon;
throwing off its moorings,
a boat sails on the sea.
Playing the lute, reciting verse,
groves of bamboo for company,
the rocks are my companions.
To those of humble estate,
honor is simply unreal;
for those without ambition,
money has no appeal.
Filling the goblet, spring wine's green;
beneath the moon, night music's serene.
Beyond the flagstone walk
is a pond that's crystal clear;
in its gentle flow
I see my unkempt hair.

Lying down in my bed,
I find it littered with books,
though wine has made me
light of head,
I rise and comb my locks.

To a Friend,
Feelings in Late Spring

The chatter of the nightingale
disrupts fragmented dreams;
a light dusting of powder
hides a face tear-stained.
In the shadow of bamboos,
the early moon is thin;
over the quiet of the river,
the evening mist is thick.
Wetting its beak
is a swallow gathering mud;
perfuming its whiskers
is a bee collecting nectar.
Alone and forlorn
as I endlessly long,
in the drooping pines
I finish my song.

Following up Another's Verse

How clamorous the crowds around
the rich and influential;
by myself, I sing alone
in the light of the moon.
What motivates the man to come
with poetry in mind?
Here he shows up at my door
with his elegant rhymes.
I chant among the jasmines
and hide in poverty:
above the pines are mountains yet;
don't seek me ardently.

Selling Leftover Peonies

Heaving a sigh in the wind,
the flower petals keep falling;
when vernal feelings have faded away,
again there comes the spring.
Is it because the price is high
that no one has inquired?
It seems the fragrance is so strong
that butterflies cannot approach!
Such crimson blossoms are only fit
to grow on palace grounds;
how could the emerald leaves
endure the dust of the road?
Once they've been planted
in a royal garden,
the scions of nobility
will have no way to buy them.

Saying Goodbye

Seeing you off day after day,
my tears roll down like florets;
I've used up all my farewells
in the misty haze
as the willows sway
in the spring breeze.
I wish I'd find a paradise
where people never part,
so they will never have to cry
these tears that drain the heart.

To a Singer

Drunken she bemoans her fate
from morning until night;
longing for another,
whom can she tell of her plight?
A letter comes in the rain,
a heart breaks by the window.
Gazing into the mountains
as she rolls up the blind,
along with the fragrant grasses
sadness comes to mind.
How many times
since we've been apart
have your clear songs
filled the air?

Thoughts on a Winter Night

With painful thoughts I reach for verse
to read aloud by the lamp;
I do not sleep the long night,
fearful of frigid bedding.
A sad wind rises in the leaves
filling the yard outside;
regrettably, the moon has set
beyond the window screen.
My hope for freedom has after all
never been quite fulfilled;
through ups and downs I see in vain
my true original will.
To live in hiding, do not choose
a place in easy reach;
evening sparrows twittering
circle the woods and screech.

To My Love Across the River

Wistfully I gaze
o'er the river,
north and south;
empty songs of longing
echo memories.
Mandarin ducks laze cozily
by the sandy beach;
water birds wing lazily
through an orange grove.
In the mist
the voice of song
is hidden subtly;
at the ford
the light of the moon
sinks deep into the waves.
I'm full of emotion
so near to you
and yet so far away,
harder to bear
whenever I hear
the distant sounds of families
on their laundry day.

Matching Rhymes with a Friend

What can dispel the sadness
of a travelers' inn?
Opening a crimson letter,
 I find elegant writing within.
When rain washes over
the mystic mountains,
the thousand peaks seem small;
when wind blows through
the northern ravines,
myriad leaves sense fall.
Every word I read by day
makes emerald jade worth less;
each poem I recite by night
is done in my bed as I rest.
Reaching for a fragrant box
to put your letter away,
I take this precious time to sing
of receiving it today.

Feelings for Another

Lodging my regrets
in the strings of my lute,
I keep feelings to myself
and do not let them out.
Though I know erotic arts
I still haven't fallen in love.
Like a beautiful peach or a plum,
I may be sought by all in the land,
but still I envy the honors
that are given to only a man.
The moonlight clean on the mossy stairs,
from the bamboo grove a song appears.
I do not sweep the crimson leaves
that lie before my door,
because I'm waiting patiently
for my paramour.

A Message Arrives

Living quietly writing verse,
how many years have I sorrowed;
my former haunt used to be a place
in a mountain range's shadow.
I sing poems east and west,
in the chaos of a thousand peaks;
horses travel north and south,
where flows a single riverlet.
Once upon a rainy night
we shared a happy time;
since we parted,
in the spring
I go upstairs alone.
A sudden delight knocks at my door
with a message of sympathy
for the dismal seclusion of my room
in this alleyway.
When one's lover's music ends,
the strings of the lute are cut;
when paired swallows leave the nest,
autumn's white with frost.

Two Verses,
On Winning a Degree and On Mourning

1
Our destiny in the human world
is not for a lengthy stay;
in but a moment, ten autumns
have already passed away.
Below the scroll of mandarin ducks,
the censer is still warm;
while in the parrot cage
chatter still goes on.
Morning dewdrops dot the flowers
like tears on a mournful face;
willows sway in the evening breeze
like brows of sorrowful eyes.
No more news is ever heard
once someone's passed away;
even successful, passionate ones
all are turning grey.
Don't be loathe to visit me
in my humble apartment;
every spring there's plenty to do
at the scenic gardens.

2

A laurel branch stands out alone
distinguished in the mist;
myriad riverside peach trees
are crimson in the rain.
Drunk before the wine jar,
let me give up wishful thinking;
sorrows and joys since ancient times
are still the same today.

A Love Note

Living a simple life
in austere faithfulness
my aim has no connection
with ordinary success.
Still there in my dreams
remains the scenery of yore,
rivers and mountains of the West
where we were before.
Now the mirror of our union
lies broken on the floor;
as I was going to strum the lute,
my lover was there no more.
By the well, the autumn leaves
make the fall rain cry;
by the window, early dawn breeze
makes the silver lamp die.
Where in the world can I ever inquire
where your letters are?
By the azure river I wait all day
for news of you from afar.